Wait! WHA

AMELIA EARHART Is on the Moon?

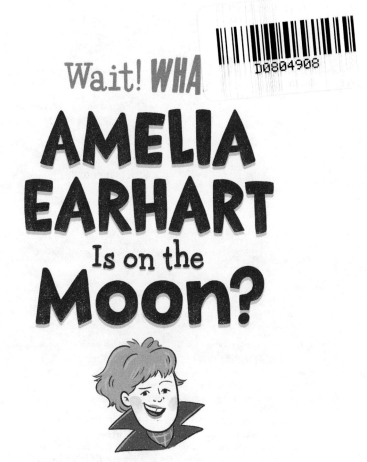

DAN GUTMAN

illustrated by **ALLISON STEINFELD**

NORTON YOUNG READERS

An Imprint of W. W. Norton & Company
Independent Publishers Since 1923

To kids who like to learn cool stuff.

For information about permission to reproduce selections from this book, write to
Permissions, W. W. Norton & Company, Inc., 500 Fifth Avenue, New York, NY 10110

For information about special discounts for bulk purchases, please contact
W. W. Norton Special Sales at specialsales@wwnorton.com or 800-233-4830

Manufacturing by Sheridan
Book design by Patrick Collins
Production manager: Anna Oler

Library of Congress Cataloging-in-Publication Data

Names: Gutman, Dan, author. | Steinfeld, Allison, illustrator.
Title: Amelia Earhart is on the moon? / Dan Gutman ; illustrated by Allison Steinfeld.
Description: First edition. | New York : Norton Young Readers, [2021] |
Series: Wait! what? | Audience: Ages 6–8
Identifiers: LCCN 2021019725 | ISBN 9781324015628 (hardcover) |
ISBN 9781324017073 (paperback) | ISBN 9781324015635 (epub)
Subjects: LCSH: Earhart, Amelia, 1897–1937—Juvenile literature. |
Women air pilots—United States—Biography—Juvenile literature. |
Air pilots—United States—Biography—Juvenile literature.
Classification: LCC TL540.E3 G88 2021 | DDC 629.13092 [B]—dc23
LC record available at https://lccn.loc.gov/2021019725

W. W. Norton & Company, Inc.
500 Fifth Avenue, New York, N.Y. 10110
www.wwnorton.com

W. W. Norton & Company Ltd.
15 Carlisle Street, London W1D 3BS

2 4 6 8 9 0 7 5 3 1

CONTENTS

Introduction: The History Mystery 1

Chapter 1: Stuff Your Teacher Wants You to
Know About Amelia Earhart... 5

Chapter 2: Worm Races and
Imaginary Monsters 8

Chapter 3: What Do You Want to Be
When You Grow Up? 20

Chapter 4: The Early Days of Flying 25

Chapter 5: A Sack of Potatoes 33

Chapter 6: Getting Famous 41

Chapter 7: R-E-S-P-E-C-T 49

Chapter 8: Getting MORE Famous 58

Chapter 9: One More Good Flight 66

Chapter 10: The Last Leg 76

Chapter 11: So What Really Happened?   86

Chapter 12: Getting Even *MORE* Famous   93

Chapter 13: Oh Yeah? (Stuff About Earhart
              That Didn't Fit Anywhere Else)   98

              To Find Out More...   104

              Acknowledgments   105

The History Mystery

Hi everybody. I'm Paige, and this is my little brother Turner. Do you want to know what's really interesting?

Yeah, Bluetooth. Why do they call it Bluetooth?

No! What's really interesting is famous people. I've read so many biographies of famous people, but they always leave out the cool stuff. The strange stuff.

So Turner and I decided to write about them. But we leave out the boring parts and include just the cool stuff.

Who's our subject this time, Paige?

You know who it is! We just spent months learning about her! She's right on the cover of the book!

 Okay, okay! Relax. I was just trying to make chitchat.

 Amelia Earhart was a pilot, and one of the most famous women in history. We did a lot of research on her. Now it's time for us to compare notes.

 Right. What she said.

 I'll tell you what I like most about Amelia Earhart—she was famous for what she accomplished, not because of the person she married or what she looked like. That stuff shouldn't matter.

Yeah, but to be honest, Amelia Earhart was most famous for something else—she disappeared! She took off in a plane one day, and it never landed. It's probably the biggest mystery in history. Hey, that rhymes! I'm a poet and I don't know it!

 It's true. She vanished off the face of the earth, and nobody knows what happened to her.

 Actually, I know what happened to her.

 You do not.

 Do too.

 Well, what happened, genius?

You think I'm going to tell you this early in the book? I'll tell you later.

Oh *sure* you will! Because you don't know.

 Says *you*. I know. I could say it right now. But I'm going to keep you in suspense.

 You're impossible!

CHAPTER 1

Stuff Your Teacher Wants You to Know About Amelia Earhart…

July 24, 1897 Born in Atchison, Kansas.

1916 Graduates from Hyde Park High School in Chicago.

1916–1919 Attends Ogontz School in Pennsylvania and Columbia University in New York.

1920 Takes her first flying lesson.

1921 Buys her first plane.

1922 Sets world altitude record for women—fourteen thousand feet.

1928 Becomes the first woman to fly across the Atlantic Ocean.

1930 Sets three records in two weeks, pushing the women's world speed record up to 181 miles per hour.

1931 Gets married to George Putnam.

1932 Becomes the first woman to fly *solo* across the Atlantic, and the first woman to receive the Distinguished Flying Cross.

1933 Becomes the first woman to fly nonstop across the United States.

1935 Becomes the first person to fly solo from Hawaii to California, the first to fly solo nonstop from California to Mexico City, and the first to fly solo nonstop from Mexico City to New Jersey.

1937 Begins an around-the-world flight on May 21. Disappears on July 2.

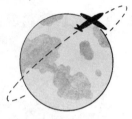

Still awake? Great! Okay, let's get to the *good* stuff, the stuff your *teacher* doesn't even know about Amelia Earhart . . .

CHAPTER 2

Worm Races and Imaginary Monsters

 Hey, Paige. I bet you don't know why her parents named her Amelia.

 I bet I *do*.

 Well, I'm gonna tell you anyway. Her grandmother's name was Amelia, and it was a family tradition to name babies after their grandparents.

I knew that. Her little sister Muriel couldn't say "Amelia," so she called her "Meeley." Amelia called Muriel "Pidge" and sometimes "Snappy." Do you know what Amelia and Muriel used to do for fun?

Ride bikes? Play with dolls? Bake cookies?

They held worm races.

Wow. That must have been *seriously* boring. I'm glad the internet was invented by the time we were born.

I've been training for weeks!

In those days, kids had to use their imaginations. There were a bunch of other girls in the neighborhood, and Amelia was their ringleader. The girls would go into a barn with a carriage in it and play a game they called Bogie.

How do you play that?

They would pretend the carriage was a magical chariot that could go all over the world. They'd have imaginary adventures where they got attacked by giant spiders, snakes, witches, ghosts, and hairy men. When they had an

adventure in Africa,
they would pretend
the carriage was an
elephant or a camel.

 That sounds cool.

 Amelia had a wild
imagination. She had
imaginary friends named Laura and Ringa, and
imaginary creatures called Dee-Jays. When her
parents caught her misbehaving, she would
blame it on the Dee-Jays. The Earhart sisters
also had imaginary horses named Beezlebub and
Saladin.

 Amelia loved books even before she knew how
to read. Her mother would read to her as long
as she was drinking a glass of milk. So Amelia
would drink the milk *very* slowly and make a
glass last an hour, to keep her mother reading.

 I used to do that with Mom and Dad.

 She also loved poetry, and she could recite parts
of *Alice in Wonderland* by heart. Here's a poem
she wrote when she was a kid . . .

"I watch the birds flying all day long
And I want to fly too.
Don't they look down sometimes, I wonder,
And wish they were me."

Amelia Loved Animals

 Amelia and Muriel had a gray cat named Von Sol and a big black dog named James Ferocious. Amelia collected spiders, moths, katydids, and toads. The sisters also had wooden animals: Amelia had a donkey named Donk and her sister had Ellie the elephant. Later in life, Amelia had canaries.

She wouldn't hurt a fly. I'm not kidding. She would actually catch flies and set them free outside.

When she became a grown-up, if Amelia was

11

driving somewhere and saw an injured animal at the side of the road, she would bring the animal to the next town and try to find someone to take care of it.

 One time Amelia found the bones of three cows that died in a blizzard. She spent hours trying to combine them into one complete cow skeleton. People started calling her Dr. Bones.

 Can you name three animals Amelia didn't like?

 Uh, rats?

 That's one. One Christmas her father gave her a .22 rifle. She used it to shoot rats. But she also hated snakes, because she thought they hurt horses. And she didn't like chickens either. A neighbor's chickens were ruining her flower garden. So she built a chicken trap out of an orange crate to stop them.

Daredevil

 Amelia Earhart was a daredevil.

 No surprise there.

I mean, even as a *kid* she did dangerous stuff. When she was seven, Amelia got a sled for Christmas. There was a big hill near her grandparents' house. So she went up to the top of the hill and jumped on the sled, belly-slammer-style.

 I know this story. The hill was icy. Amelia picked up speed. Suddenly she noticed a junk man's horse was crossing the road right in front of her. She couldn't turn. She couldn't stop. She shouted, but the junk man couldn't hear her. Do you know what happened next?

 She disappeared and was never seen again?

 No! She put her head down and slid right under the horse's belly, between its front and back legs.

 Awesome!

 Around the same time, her family took a trip to the World's Fair in St. Louis. Amelia wanted to ride the roller coaster, but her mother wouldn't let her. So when Amelia got home, she and her friends built a roller coaster in the backyard.

 How do you build a roller coaster?

 By taking two long strips of wood, greasing them with lard, and nailing them to the roof of the garage. Then Amelia attached roller-skate wheels to a big wooden box, dragged it up to the top, and climbed into the box.

 That sounds more dangerous than a *real* roller coaster.

 It was. Amelia went head over heels, cut her lip, and tore her dress. But she loved it. "Oh, Pidge," she told her sister, "it's just like flying!"

I'm free!

BOING!

CRASH!

Climbing

Long before Amelia ever got on a plane, she loved heights. Her grandmother used to tell her, "Ladies don't climb fences, child." But Amelia couldn't help herself.

One time her cat went missing while the family was moving from one house to another in the same town. Amelia and Muriel sneaked back to their old house that night with a sack. They found the cat, but it scrambled up into a tree. So Amelia climbed up on the roof, hopped into the tree, and grabbed the cat to bring it home.

GOTCHA!

When she was in college, Amelia climbed up to the top of the dome of the library just for the fun of it. It was the highest point

15

on the campus. The students below saw her and applauded.

 Hey, maybe Amelia's love of high places came from her mother. She was the first woman to climb Pikes Peak in Colorado.

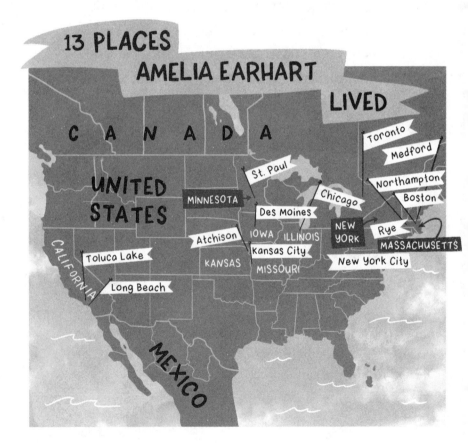

13 PLACES AMELIA EARHART LIVED

CANADA

UNITED STATES

CALIFORNIA

Toluca Lake

Long Beach

MINNESOTA

St. Paul

Des Moines

Atchison

IOWA

ILLINOIS

Kansas City

KANSAS

MISSOURI

Chicago

NEW YORK

New York City

Toronto

Medford

Northampton

Boston

Rye

MASSACHUSETTS

MEXICO

Money

 Amelia's father was a lawyer who worked for the railroad. He didn't make a lot of money, but he got free train tickets. That's one reason why the Earhart family moved around a lot.

 The other reason they moved so much is because her dad was an alcoholic. He had trouble holding a job.

 I wasn't going to go there, but it's true. Her father wasn't a successful lawyer. At one point, he thought he could make a fortune by inventing a flag holder for a train caboose. He traveled all the way to Washington to get it patented. But when he got there, he discovered that somebody had invented the same thing two years earlier.

 Ouch! Burn!

 Money was such a problem that the Earharts would close off half the rooms of their house during the winter to reduce the heating bills.

 Actually, Amelia spent much of her childhood living with her grandmother. Amelia was homeschooled, and didn't go to public school until seventh grade.

 Okay, enough of this kiddie stuff. Let's move on.

 Wait. We didn't talk about what Amelia looked like.

 Who cares? If she was a man, you wouldn't ask what she looked like.

 No, I'd ask what *he* looked like! Chillax, will you? I just want to form a mental picture. I know from pictures that she had short blond hair, and she had freckles.

 She was athletic. She liked swimming, fencing, and playing basketball. She was so flexible that she could stand up, lean forward, and put both of her palms on the ground without bending her knees.

Wow, I can't do that.

 She didn't like her legs, and she wore pants most of the time to hide them. Amelia was tall and very skinny. Sometimes she would eat waffles soaked in butter, trying to gain weight.

 Yum!

"ADVENTURE IS WORTHWHILE IN ITSELF."

CHAPTER 3

What Do You Want to Be When You Grow Up?

 A hundred years ago, girls were expected to grow up and find a husband, get married, have kids, and take care of their home. But that wasn't for Amelia. She wanted to be a doctor.

She was interested in science, but the high school near her home in Chicago had a chemistry lab that was no better than a kitchen sink. So Amelia went to Hyde Park High School instead.

 She wasn't popular in high school. She thought her English teacher was terrible, so she made a petition demanding that the teacher get fired. Her classmates tore it up.

 Ouch! *Burn.* I guess she didn't make a lot of friends.

 No. In her yearbook, it said, "A.E.—the girl in brown who walks alone." She didn't go to her graduation. She didn't even pick up her diploma.

Peter Daniels
Class President

Sigh.

Amelia Earhart
The girl in brown
Who walks alone

Beatrice Earl
Glee Club

College was better. Amelia was the vice president of her class, played field hockey, and even wrote the senior class song. She went to Ogontz, a two-year college near Philadelphia. It was named after a Native American chief.

 Ogontz was called a "finishing school." Besides all the usual subjects, the students were also taught how to behave—how to walk, bow, shake hands, and even sit on a chair correctly!

 You could go to college to learn how to sit on a chair? I would have gone to that school.

 No, you wouldn't. It was an all-girls school. After Ogontz, Amelia went to Columbia University in New York to study medicine. But the school was too expensive for her family, and she decided she didn't want to be a doctor after all.

 So she never finished college.

 Right. Amelia was a little lost. She didn't know what to do with her life. She went to visit her sister, who was living in Toronto. World War I had started, and Amelia saw wounded soldiers

"I believe that a girl should not do what she thinks she should do, but should find out through experience what she wants to do."

who were home from the war. Many were on crutches. Some had lost an arm or leg. Amelia felt bad for them and decided to become a nurse's aide.

 She also decided that she was a pacifist. That's somebody who's against war or violence as a way to settle arguments.

When the war ended in 1918, the Spanish flu epidemic sweeping the world had killed millions of people. Amelia was almost one of them. She got a sinus infection, caught pneumonia, and was sent to the hospital. There were no antibiotics back then. She had operations and suffered from sinus problems her whole life. Sometimes she wore a bandage on her cheek to hide a drainage tube.

 Yikes! Around that time, Amelia got a job as a teacher and social worker in Boston. She liked it and was good at it. She was patient and enjoyed working with people, who were mostly Chinese and Syrian immigrants. She also liked working with kids—reading to them, playing games, and teaching English. It looked like she might have a career in social work.

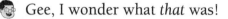

 But then she got interested in something else.

 Gee, I wonder what *that* was!

 Let's tell them in the next chapter.

CHAPTER 4

The Early Days of Flying

 When Amelia was born, the airplane hadn't even been *invented* yet. She was six when the Wright Brothers got off the ground in 1903.

She didn't see her first plane until she was ten, when her family went to the Iowa State Fair. Her dad asked her if she wanted to go on an airplane ride. But Amelia took one look at the flimsy "flying machine" and decided to ride on a merry-go-round instead.

In those days, just *seeing* a plane must have blown people's minds! They would pay money to go to an "air circus" and watch World War I fighter pilots dive, spin, fly upside down, do barrel rolls, and put on fake dogfights. Sometimes they would skywrite or walk out on the wing of the plane while it was flying.

In St. Louis, a cow was sent up in a plane and *milked* while it was in the air! Then the milk was put in containers and the pilot dropped them down to the crowd with little parachutes. Cool!

One day in 1918, Amelia went to an air show in Toronto. She and a friend were standing at the edge of the field. One of the pilots spotted them and decided to have a little fun by diving his plane right at them. Amelia's friend ran out of the way. But Amelia didn't budge. She said, "I believe that little red airplane said something to me as it swished by."

On Christmas day in 1920, Amelia and her father went to an airfield in Long Beach, California. She was twenty-three. He paid ten dollars—a lot of money back then—so she could take her first ride in a plane. She was hooked.

"As soon as we left the ground, I knew I myself had to fly."

Remember, up until that year women weren't even allowed to *vote*. A woman piloting a plane was *really* unusual. But Amelia was determined. She saved a thousand dollars to pay for flying lessons. She had to walk three miles to the airfield for them.

 She even found one of the few female flight instructors, Anita Snook. Anita took Amelia up in a "Canuck"—a plane that had no gas gauge, no brakes, and instead of a rear wheel it had a skid that dragged on the ground to slow it down after it landed. After two hours of lessons, Amelia decided to buy a plane of her own.

 World War I was over by that time, and there were plenty of used planes for sale. They were even advertised in magazines. You could buy a pair of wings for twenty dollars, an engine for eighty-five, and a cheap plane for less than a thousand.

 For her twenty-fourth birthday in 1921, Amelia bought a Kinner Airster. Her mother helped pay the two-thousand-dollar price. It was a biplane, which meant it had two sets of wings on each side. The Airster had a top speed of ninety miles an hour, not much faster than a car. The whole thing weighed just six hundred pounds. You could pick it up by the tail and roll it around.

 Amelia had the Airster painted yellow and named it *The Canary*.

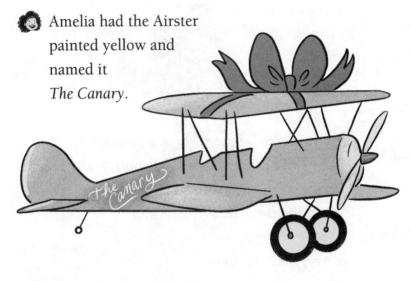

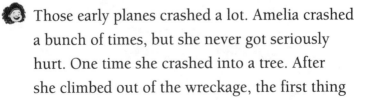 Here's a not-so-fun fact I found: A year later, Amelia sold *The Canary* to a guy who had just started flying. The first time he took it up, he crashed, killing himself and a passenger.

 Those early planes crashed a lot. Amelia crashed a bunch of times, but she never got seriously hurt. One time she crashed into a tree. After she climbed out of the wreckage, the first thing she did was powder her nose. She said she wanted to look nice when the reporters showed up.

I'm ready for my close-up!

But she was getting good at flying. She learned how to do steep banked turns, dives, tailspins, and loops. These weren't just stunts to show off. Mastering them helped pilots learn how to get out of dangerous situations.

Amelia had her first solo flight in December 1921. Just ten months later, she set the world altitude record for female pilots—fourteen thousand feet.

 I wonder how they measured that.

 Good question. Her plane had this thing called a barograph. It measured atmospheric pressure. The pressure changes depending on the distance above sea level, so a barograph could measure altitude.

 Amelia wanted to look like a regular pilot, so she bought herself a leather jacket. She didn't want it to look brand-new, so she slept in it for three nights and rubbed oil into it to make it look old and worn. Today, that jacket is at the National Air and Space Museum in Washington.

Paying the Bills

 Flying was an expensive hobby. Planes cost a lot of money to buy, repair, and store in a garage. Amelia had to work to pay her bills, and she did her flying on the weekends. She would have liked to earn a living as a pilot, but there were no airlines yet. There wasn't a lot of opportunity for pilots, and especially lady pilots.

 She had lots of jobs. She was a telephone operator and a stenographer for a while. She learned about photography and worked in a photo studio. Guess what she liked to take pictures of?

 Airplanes?

 No, garbage cans.

 That was my next guess.

 It's true! She also took a class in auto mechanics and became a truck driver for a while, hauling sand and gravel. Later, she worked as a sales representative, newspaper writer, magazine editor, lecturer, author, airline executive, women's career counselor, and she even owned a flying school.

CHAPTER 5

A Sack of Potatoes

 In 1927, Charles Lindbergh became the first person to pilot an airplane solo—alone—across the Atlantic Ocean. He became an instant American hero, and one of the most famous men in the world.

A year later, Amelia was working as a social worker in Boston when she was asked if she'd like to be the first *woman* to fly across the Atlantic.

She wouldn't be the pilot. The pilot was twenty-eight-year-old Wilmer "Bill" Stultz. And she wouldn't be the co-pilot either. That was mechanic Louis "Slim" Gordon, who was twenty-seven. Amelia would just be a passenger who kept the flight log. She said yes.

 Later, she wrote, "I was just baggage, like a sack of potatoes."

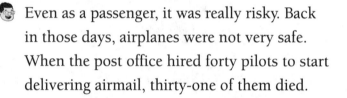 Even as a passenger, it was really risky. Back in those days, airplanes were not very safe. When the post office hired forty pilots to start delivering airmail, thirty-one of them died.

And that was flying over *land*. You could at least *land* on land! In the year after Lindbergh's flight, fourteen pilots died trying to fly across the ocean.

 Three of those pilots who died were women. Lots of female pilots wanted to be the first to cross the Atlantic. It was a race. And nobody cares about who finishes *second* in a race.

I bet the danger was one of the reasons people wanted to be pilots in the first place.

Amelia didn't tell anyone about the flight in advance, not even her family. She made out her will and wrote a letter to her parents in case she didn't make it . . .

"Even though I have lost, the adventure was worth while...My life has really been very happy, and I don't mind contemplating its end in the midst of it."

The plane was called *Friendship*. It was a Fokker, and the outside skin was made of plywood. It was painted bright orange, so it could be seen from a distance. The wings were gold.

 Instead of wheels, the *Friendship* had pontoons—big floats, sort of like canoes. So the plane could land on water.

 Of course, it also had to *take off* from water. It was the first pontoon plane to attempt a transatlantic flight.

 Friendship had a top speed of 129 miles per hour, and it could hold 872 gallons of gas. Gee, I wonder how much gas a car can hold.

Small cars hold about twelve gallons. Bigger cars can hold sixteen gallons.

How much does a gallon of gas weigh?

About six pounds. So they had to get off the ground carrying over five *thousand* pounds of gas.

Wow. How do you know that?

What do you think? I looked it up. The plane was like a flying gas tank! It didn't even have seats in the back. Amelia sat on a gas can.

That's why they had trouble taking off from Newfoundland, Canada. The plane was too heavy. So Bill, Slim, and Amelia got rid of their movie camera, film, a thermos, extra clothing, and as much gas as they could spare.

After eleven failed attempts, the plane lifted off the water. It looked like smooth sailing, but as they took off, the cabin door suddenly swung open. Amelia and Slim Gordon almost fell out! The lock on the door was broken. They tied it closed with a rope.

There were more problems. After the first hour, they ran into a thunderstorm. They couldn't get above or around it. For the next nineteen hours, they flew through thick fog. They couldn't see anything in front of them. They weren't sure where they were. And gas was running low.

Finally, they saw a ship below, and circled over it. Amelia wrote a note asking for the ship's position. She tied the note to an orange and tried to drop it on the ship's deck. But she missed. She tried again with another orange, and missed again.

 The captain of the ship rushed to write the ship's name and position in big chalk letters on the deck. But the crew of the *Friendship* couldn't keep circling around to see it. The engines burned thirty-three gallons of gas each hour, and the tank was just about empty. They had to keep going until they reached land.

 After twenty hours of flying, they spotted a blue shadow in the distance. It was the coast of South Wales. When they landed, the gas gauge was on empty.

Whew! Exciting!

Right?

I bet you're wondering how Amelia went to the bathroom if she was flying for so many hours.

I wasn't wondering that.

Sure you were.

Turner, I don't want to hear it.

39

She used a funnel and a pail.

 Please stop.

 Oh, and Amelia wore men's underwear to make it easier for her to use the bathroom. It's true!

 Okay, let's move on.

"When a grand adventure is offered to you — you don't refuse it, that's all."

CHAPTER 6

Getting Famous

Bill, Slim, and Amelia sat there floating on the water for almost an hour. But when they got on dry land, bam! Hundreds of people surrounded them, pushing and shoving. Everybody wanted to touch Amelia, get her autograph, or just get a *look* at her. Somebody grabbed the scarf she was wearing and took it as a souvenir.

She may have been a sack of potatoes, but Amelia was a hero. The flight became worldwide news. Every newspaper covered the story. Amelia was nicknamed "Lady Lindy." People even said she *looked* like Charles Lindbergh. She was invited to dance with the Prince of Wales. In England she had tea at the House of Commons.

 When she got home, it was Amelia-mania! Five thousand people greeted her when her ship docked in New York. Bands played. There was a ticker tape parade. She met Babe Ruth, and visited President Calvin Coolidge at the White House. She went to a celebration of the 25th anniversary of the first flight with Orville Wright.

 Amelia made people—especially women— proud to be American. She was America's sweetheart. Men asked her to marry them.

Meanwhile, just about everybody ignored the *real* pilots of the *Friendship*, Bill Stultz and Slim Gordon. It bothered Amelia. She knew she didn't deserve so much attention.

At one event in Chicago, Bill and Slim couldn't be there. Two *other* guys took their places sitting next to Amelia, and nobody knew the difference. Bill Stultz and Slim Gordon became a trivia question nobody could answer.

This is even sadder. Less than a year later, Bill Stultz and two of his passengers were killed when a stunt plane he was piloting crashed on Long Island.

GP

Amelia would have been famous no matter what. But it helped that the mastermind behind the Atlantic flight was a guy named George Palmer Putnam. "GP" is a big part of the Amelia Earhart story.

He was the grandson of the guy who started the G. P. Putnam's Sons book company. After publishing Charles Lindbergh's book *"WE,"* GP wanted to find a woman to do what Lindbergh had done. He needed a woman who was educated, had manners, and was good-looking. Oh, and it would help if she knew how to pilot a plane.

 GP found Amelia and had her write a book about the flight—*20 Hrs. 40 Min.: Our Flight in the Friendship*. She started writing the book while the plane was still in the air, and finished it two weeks after she got home.

 But GP did more than just publish Amelia's book. He also showed her how to be a celebrity. He taught her how to talk into a microphone. He told her to keep her mouth closed when

Not so loud!

she was getting her picture taken so the gap between her teeth wouldn't show. They say he was even responsible for her hairstyle.

Perfect!

GP told Amelia that she didn't look good in hats, so she hardly ever wore one. "Your hats!" he said. "They are a public menace. You should do something about them when you must wear them at all!"

Man, GP sounds like a jerk.

"The woman who can create her own job is the woman who will win fame and fortune."

 I don't know about that. But here's the most interesting part of the story. The whole time GP was making Amelia famous, he was also falling in love with her!

I wasn't going to go there.

We have to! For seven years, Amelia had been dating a guy from Boston named Sam Chapman. They were engaged to be married in 1928, even though Amelia had problems with the idea of marrying *anyone*.

"I am still unsold on marriage," she wrote.

"I think I may not ever be able to see marriage except as a cage." She said it would take more courage to get married that it took to cross the Atlantic in a plane.

 But then she met GP. He asked her to marry him *six* times. Finally she said yes, and they got married in 1931.

 It was an unusual marriage for back then. Amelia never wore her wedding ring. They never had kids together. She kept her own name.

In the newspapers, Amelia was sometimes called "Mrs. Putnam." She didn't like that. But sometimes GP was called "Mr. Earhart."

The day before their wedding, Amelia wrote a letter to GP saying it would be a trial marriage. She wrote: "I must exact a cruel promise, and that is that you will let me go in a year if we find no happiness together."

 GP was okay with that. The marriage lasted six years, until the day Amelia disappeared.

Did they really love each other? Who knows? But there's one thing GP loved about Amelia— her hands! He put a full-page photo of them in his autobiography. He wrote, "The tapering loveliness of her hands was almost unbelievable."

 That's weird. So whatever happened to Amelia's old boyfriend Sam Chapman?

He never did get married. Maybe he never got over Amelia.

BETCHA DIDN'T KNOW: GP's first wife, Dorothy, was the daughter of Edwin Binney, an inventor of Crayola crayons!

CHAPTER 7

R-E-S-P-E-C-T

 Not *everyone* was so impressed that Amelia crossed the Atlantic. One newspaper wrote, "Her presence added no more to the achievement than if the passenger had been a sheep."

There were a *lot* of great female pilots in those days—Louise Thaden, Ruth Nichols, Elinor Smith, Bessie Coleman, and others. But they didn't get as much attention because none of them had flown across the ocean. Amelia knew she hadn't earned her fame. She knew people were whispering that she wasn't a great pilot. She wanted to earn respect.

 The way to get it back then was to set records. Everybody wanted to fly higher, faster, or farther. To set a record, you needed a cool plane. Amelia got herself a Lockheed Vega. It had a two-hundred-horsepower engine, and was built for speed and long distance. It looked like a bullet.

Amelia began setting records. In 1928, she became the first woman to fly solo across North America and back. In 1931, she set the world altitude record— 18,415 feet.

That's like fourteen Empire State Buildings stacked on top of each other!

Between 1930 and 1935, she set seven women's speed and distance records. She was gaining fame *and* respect.

Maybe you should talk about the women's movement stuff.

Why me? Just because I'm a girl?

Well, yeah.

Well, okay! When Amelia was our age, there were no female senators or state governors. Women couldn't *vote*. But Amelia wanted to do great things, and she wanted other women to do great things too.

As a kid, she made a scrapbook filled with newspaper articles about successful women: The state's only female bank president. The only woman in the Federal Forestry Service. The first woman in India to become a lawyer.

As she grew up and got famous, she used her fame to tell women they could be what they want to be and do what they want to do. She told girls to graduate from school, start a career, and *then* get married if they wanted to. She said we could end wars if women joined the military. She supported the Equal Rights Amendment, which would have changed the Constitution to say that men and women are equal.

If they can do it, I can too!

They *still* haven't passed the ERA.

I know. And it makes me mad! Amelia was also one of the founders of the Ninety-Nines, an organization of female pilots.

I know why it was called the Ninety-Nines. Because that's the number of members it had at the beginning. And today they have over six *thousand*.

Speaking of the Ninety-Nines, in 1929 there was a race just for female pilots. The first woman to fly from California to Cleveland, Ohio, would win eight thousand dollars. The race was officially called the Women's Air Derby. But Will Rogers nicknamed it the Powder Puff Derby, and that name stuck. Nineteen women entered the race. Sixteen finished. Three of the planes crashed. One pilot, Marvel Crosson, died. Amelia came in third.

Going Solo

But there was *another* race going on—the race to be the first woman to fly *solo* across the Atlantic. All the top female pilots wanted to do what Lindbergh had done. In May 1932, Amelia was ready to go. It was the fifth anniversary of Lindbergh's flight.

To practice for this flight, Amelia's Vega was loaded with sandbags to see how much gas it could carry. She couldn't land with all that weight, so she dropped the sandbags one by one. It looked like the plane was dropping bombs.

Here's a great fact: One of the people who helped prepare Amelia's plane for this flight was Major Edwin Aldrin. His son was Buzz Aldrin, the astronaut who would walk on the moon thirty-seven years later.

 Amelia packed a comb, a toothbrush, tomato juice, and chicken soup. She didn't bring a parachute, because of the weight.

 She started flying east across the Atlantic from Newfoundland, and things started going wrong almost right away. One hour into the trip, the altimeter stopped working. So she didn't know how high she was flying.

 Three hours in, she smelled burning oil. There were gas fumes in the cockpit. Gas was dripping on the back of her neck! She looked out the window and saw blue flames coming out of the engine! But she had gone too far to turn back.

 Four hours into the trip, she ran into a storm. When she climbed to get over it, ice formed on the wings. When she flew lower to melt the ice, she nearly hit the water. Oh, and the fuel gauge broke too.

It was ten more
hours like
that. Finally
she reached
Ireland, landing
the plane in a
pasture. She had become
the first woman to fly solo across the Atlantic,
and also the first person to fly across it twice.

There weren't many people around. Some cows
scattered to get out of the way. Later, rumors
spread that Amelia killed a cow. She said that
was only possible if the cow died from fright.

A man came over to the plane and Amelia
asked him where she was.

"You're in Derry," he replied. "Have you
flown far?"

"From America."

CHAPTER 8

Getting MORE Famous

 The news that a woman had flown across the ocean all by herself spread around the world almost *instantly*. Amelia became even more famous than she was before.

 She was a rock star before there was rock!

There were parades, honors, and lots of opportunities to make money. George Putnam—GP—who was now her husband, was all over them . . .

Writing!

Two weeks after Amelia got back to the United States, her second book—*The Fun of It*—came out. She was also hired to write articles for *Cosmopolitan* magazine, with titles like "Shall You Let Your Daughter Fly?" and "Why Are Women Afraid to Fly?"

Speaking!

 There was no TV in 1932. Celebrities would go on lecture tours to promote themselves. Amelia was a good speaker, and she gave 136 lectures in one year. And of course, she sold her books at each appearance.

Endorsements!

Just like today, celebrities made money by lending their names to products. Amelia endorsed her plane, propeller, spark plugs, engine, gas, oil, and navigation instruments. She also got paid to say she liked Chrysler cars, Longines watches, Kodak cameras, Bausch & Lomb sunglasses, and Beech-Nut gum.

 Amelia had her own line of suitcases—Modernaire Earhart Luggage. They were popular long after she was gone, and you can still find them on eBay today.

 Amelia didn't smoke, but she was paid fifteen hundred dollars to endorse Lucky Strike cigarettes in magazine ads. People wrote letters protesting, and the ads were discontinued. This was still before everyone knew that cigarettes cause cancer, but many people felt that "nice women don't smoke."

 When Amelia and George wanted to redo their kitchen, he got a mail-order company to pay for it. In return, the mail-order company advertised its "Amelia Earhart kitchen."

Autographs!

 Stamp collecting was really popular in the

1930s. Collectors paid a lot of money for signed envelopes with special stamps inside. Amelia would get up in the morning and autograph ten envelopes before drinking her orange juice, fifteen envelopes before eating her bacon and eggs, and twenty-five envelopes before going to sleep at night. She signed *thousands* of them.

Clothing!

As a kid, Amelia learned how to sew. She would ask her grandmother for leftover fabric to make dresses for her dolls. When she was a teenager, Amelia made skirts out of old drapes. In 1933, when she made the Ten Best-Dressed Women list, she started her own clothing line.

Amelia Earhart Fashions were dresses, blouses, pants, and hats "for the woman who lives actively." They were cheap to buy and didn't get all wrinkled. Some of the clothes were made out of parachute silk, and had propeller-shaped buttons. Amelia didn't just lend her name to the products. She actually designed them herself.

Before the 1930s, most women wore dresses all the time. It was Amelia, along with movie stars Katharine Hepburn and Marlene Dietrich, who gets credit for making it acceptable for women to wear pants.

Dumb Stunts

GP had Amelia do just about *anything* for publicity. He arranged for her to be the first female referee of the Indianapolis 500. He arranged for her to do a parachute jump from a tower in New Jersey. He even arranged for her to get arrested! It's *true*. She was pulled over for speeding, pleaded guilty, and was fined one dollar.

GP made sure to schedule Amelia's flights on Saturday afternoons. That way, articles about her would appear in the Sunday newspapers.

Amelia was so popular that sometimes things got out of control. When she landed in a new city, she had to be careful not to run over people swarming around her plane before it stopped rolling. They would climb up and walk on the wings, which were made of linen. Some people would even poke their umbrellas and pencils through the fabric.

"A single act of kindness throws out roots in all directions, and the roots spring up and make new trees. The greatest work that kindness does to others is that it makes them kind themselves."

If she can do it, I can too!

CHAPTER 9

One More Good Flight

 I guess it's time we talk about the elephant in the room.

 There's an elephant in the room?

 It's just an expression! That means there's something really obvious that we haven't been talking about—Amelia Earhart's disappearance.

Oh that. Yeah, everybody knows how this story ends. But hardly anybody knows what led up to the ending. Let's do it.

 No jokes here, okay? This is serious stuff.

 Okay! Amelia was setting all kinds of flying records in the early 1930s. But she was always looking for her next challenge. And the ultimate challenge in those days was a trip around the world.

 Amelia wasn't the first to come up with that idea. Hey, Magellan sailed around the world back in 1519.

 Or he tried to, anyway. In the Philippines, he was attacked with bamboo spears and killed.

 By Amelia Earhart's time, lots of people had already traveled all the way around the world. Before the airplane was invented, a guy named William Perry Fogg did it. He inspired the 1872

Jules Verne novel *Around the World in Eighty Days*. A few years later, Nellie Bly, a newspaper reporter, did it in seventy-two days.

 That's nothing. In 1911, a French guy named Andre Jaeger-Schmidt traveled around the world in thirty-nine days. And he only had one leg!

But we're talking about *flying* around the world. Other people beat Amelia to that too. Wiley Post flew around the world *twice*. But here's the thing—nobody had ever flown around the world *at the equator*.

We should explain that. The equator is an imaginary line that goes around the middle of the Earth. It's sort of like the planet's waistline. Amelia wanted to fly as close to the equator as possible. The entire trip would be twenty-nine thousand miles. To do that, she needed a few things . . .

A Newer, Cooler Plane

On her thirty-ninth birthday, Amelia got a Lockheed Electra 10E. It was state-of-the-art in 1937, and one of the first planes with an aluminum surface. It could fly two hundred miles an hour, and up to nineteen thousand feet high.

Plus, it had *two* engines. If you're in a single-engine plane and the engine fails while you're flying over the ocean, well, you can imagine what would happen.

The only other person who owned a Lockheed Electra 10E at the time was the multimillionaire Howard Hughes.

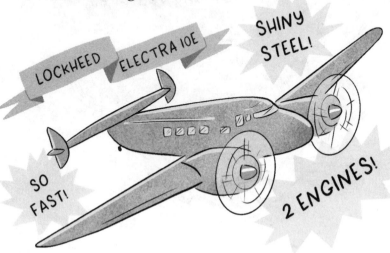

LOCKHEED ELECTRA 10E

SHINY STEEL!

SO FAST!

2 ENGINES!

The second thing Amelia needed was a good navigator. Amelia and GP hired Fred Noonan, who had already made eighteen flights across the Pacific Ocean. He was also an experienced ship captain who survived three torpedo attacks in World War I.

 Flying around the world is complicated, and it took a year to plan the trip. Amelia and Fred had to make sure there would be oil, gas, and

"Preparation, I have often said, is rightly two-thirds of any venture."

mechanics at all thirty locations where they would be stopping. They had to get permission to fly over and land in all those countries. They would need to arrange places to sleep and eat along the way.

This flight was promoted as a scientific mission, and the Lockheed was called a "flying laboratory." But some people said the whole thing was just a risky stunt, especially after the way it ended.

Takeoff

It was March 17, 1937. Amelia and Fred climbed into the Electra for the first leg of the trip, from Oakland, California, to Hawaii. Fred didn't sit next to Amelia in the cockpit. He sat behind her, in the back. It was noisy, so they communicated by writing notes on cards and passing them back and forth with a fishing pole.

That flight went off without a hitch. But then trouble began. Trying to take off in Hawaii, Amelia couldn't get the plane off the runway. It spun out and was damaged. It would take two months to repair the plane. Amelia and Fred took a ship back to California.

 While they were waiting for the plane to be fixed, Amelia made a big decision. Instead of flying *west* around the world, she would fly *east*. This was mainly to avoid monsoon season in the Caribbean and Africa.

"I have the feeling there's just one more good flight left in my system, and I hope this is it."

Okay, so they started all over again. It was May 21. Amelia and Fred took off from Oakland and headed across the United States. They were carrying life preservers, parachutes, a rubber raft, water canteens, chocolate bars, raisins, tomato juice, emergency rations, and fishing gear. They also brought a machete, in case they were forced down in a jungle.

Let me just mention that on her other flights, Amelia brought along a little silk American flag. This time, she didn't take it.

There were problems just getting across America. During a stop in Arizona, one of the engines burst into flames while the plane was on the ground. In Miami, a shock absorber had to be replaced. They fixed the problems and decided to keep going.

Around the world

If you have a map or a globe, you can follow Amelia's route: Miami, Puerto Rico, Venezuela, Brazil. Then a hop across the Atlantic to Africa—Senegal and Sudan. On to Pakistan and India.

Things were going well. Amelia got to visit some of the places she and her sister had imagined when they were kids playing Bogie

in the barn. She rode a camel, and walked on the rim of a volcano. She went deep-sea fishing.

It helped that Fred spoke some Spanish and Portuguese, and Amelia knew some French and German.

Between India and the South China Sea, they ran into monsoons. The rain beat down so hard that paint came off the wings of the plane. But Amelia and Fred pressed on. And every night, no matter how tired she was, Amelia would send a report to the *New York Herald Tribune*.

Keep following on the map—Rangoon. Singapore. Australia. New Guinea. Amelia and Fred were getting closer to their goal.

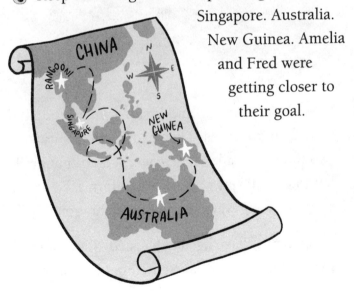

CHAPTER 10

The Last Leg

 It was July 2. Amelia and Fred rested at a hotel in Lae, New Guinea. They had flown twenty-two thousand miles. There were seven thousand left to go. GP was waiting in California, planning a big welcome-home celebration.

 Amelia must have been exhausted. She'd been flying almost every day, sometimes for thirteen hours. There had been mechanical problems, radio problems, and bad weather.

 She'd been sick from inhaling gas fumes. She had nausea and diarrhea. She sent her last article to the *Herald Tribune* . . .

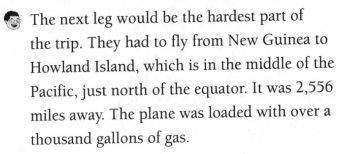

"The whole width of the world has passed behind us - except this broad ocean. I shall be glad when we have the hazards of its navigation behind us."

The next leg would be the hardest part of the trip. They had to fly from New Guinea to Howland Island, which is in the middle of the Pacific, just north of the equator. It was 2,556 miles away. The plane was loaded with over a thousand gallons of gas.

Fred and Amelia had ditched their parachutes in Australia. The rest of the trip would be over water, and there would be no point in parachuting into the ocean.

 Everybody knew it could be hard to find Howland Island. It's just two miles long and a half a mile wide. If there was a cloud below the plane, Amelia and Fred might not see it.

 But they had help. The USS *Ontario* was positioned halfway between New Guinea and Howland to guide them. The Coast Guard cutter *Itasca* was waiting near Howland. It would send up a dark column of smoke that could be seen from miles away. The *Itasca* would also communicate with Amelia by radio.

AMELIA
& FRED

HOWLAND
ISLAND
↓

NEW
GUINEA

USS ONTARIO

Radio

 If Amelia was flying today, she could pinpoint her position with GPS, just like in a car. But there was no GPS in 1937. They had radio transmitters that used various frequencies to send messages by voice or Morse code.

But Amelia and Fred barely knew Morse code, and neither of them really liked using radio communications.

Fred was an expert with an "octant," this tool that used the sun and stars to locate your position. It dated back to 1731. There was a radio on the plane too, but it wasn't a special marine-frequency radio.

The problem was, the captain of the *Itasca* didn't *know* Amelia didn't have a marine-frequency radio. He kept trying to contact her on those frequencies.

Even so, everything was fine for about 750 miles. There were some clouds, but visibility was good. At 2:45 a.m., the *Itasca* picked up a muffled report from Amelia about the weather. At 3:45 they received another one. They asked Amelia for her position, but didn't get a response.

 At 4:00, the *Itasca* radioed *"What is your position? When do you expect to arrive Howland?"* No response.

 At 4:53, the *Itasca* received a faint message from Amelia, but there was too much static to understand it.

At 6:14, Amelia radioed that she was *"about 200 miles out."*

 At 6:45, Amelia radioed that she was *"about 100 miles out."*

 There was a lighthouse on Howland Island that could be seen for miles. Three landing strips had been built on the island just for this flight. They were marked off with red flags to make them easier to see. Birds had been shooed away from the area.

 At 7:42, Amelia radioed, *"We must be on you, but cannot see you but gas is running low. Been unable to reach you by radio. We are flying at altitude 1000 feet. Only one-half hour of gas left."*

 At 7:43, Amelia radioed, *"Earhart calling Itasca. We are circling but cannot hear you."*

At 8:00, Amelia radioed, *"We received your signals but cannot get a minimum.* [That means a bearing.] *Please take bearing on us."*

In all these messages, Amelia never gave the *Itasca* her exact position, speed, course, or estimated time of arrival. By 8:15, the gas tanks should have been empty. It looked like it was all over.

 But at 8:44, Amelia radioed, *"We are on the line of position 156–137. Will repeat message. We will repeat this message on 6210 kilocycles. Wait. Listening on 6210 kilocycles. We are running north and south."*

And that was it. Amelia was never heard from again. She was three weeks away from her fortieth birthday.

Womanhunt

It was one of the biggest search-and-rescue missions in history. The crew of the *Itasca* looked for Amelia's plane near Howland Island. The Navy and Coast Guard searched all over the Pacific. Aircraft carriers, battleships, and sixty-five planes combed 250,000 square miles of the ocean with high-powered searchlights.

They found nothing.
The official search ended
on July 19, but GP didn't
give up. He offered a two-
thousand-dollar reward
for any information, and
he chartered boats to search
islands in the Pacific for any

sign of Amelia. It was a year before he would
admit that she was no longer alive.

Others Who Vanished

Amelia Earhart was the most famous missing
person in history. But there have been others.

Like Henry Hudson. He was
an English explorer, and the
Hudson River was named
after him. In 1611, his crew
had a mutiny and threw him
on a lifeboat in Canada. His
body was never found.

D. B. Cooper. In 1971, he hijacked a plane in
Seattle, demanding two hundred thousand

dollars and a parachute. He jumped out of the plane, and that was the last time anybody saw him.

 Jimmy Hoffa. He was the boss of the Teamsters Union. He disappeared without a trace from a parking lot near Detroit in 1975.

Harold Holt. He was the prime minister of Australia. One day in 1967, he went for a swim and vanished.

Theodosia Burr Alston. She was the daughter of former vice president Aaron Burr, who shot Alexander Hamilton. In 1813, she was on a ship

 from South Carolina to New York to visit her father. The ship never arrived, and was never found. There's a song about her in the Broadway show *Hamilton*.

Frank Morris and John and Clarence Anglin. They were bank robbers in jail at Alcatraz, a mile from San Francisco off the California coast. In 1962, they escaped by digging through walls with spoons and making a raft out of raincoats. Nobody knows if they survived the paddle to freedom.

 Joseph Crater. After eating lunch at a restaurant one day in 1930, the New York Supreme Court judge vanished and was never heard from again.

"It is far easier to start something than it is to finish it."

CHAPTER 11

So What Really Happened?

 Okay, I've waited long enough. What really happened to Amelia Earhart, Mr. Smart Guy?

 How should I know?

 You said you knew!

 When?

In the beginning of the book!

 Oh that. I was just joking.

 You're impossible!

 Look, *nobody* knows what happened to Amelia Earhart or Fred Noonan, or their plane. But there are three top guesses.

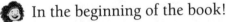

1. THEY CRASHED INTO THE PACIFIC AND SANK.

 This one makes the most sense. Amelia and Fred ran out of gas searching for Howland Island. They hit the water and sank seventeen thousand feet below the surface. The plane is still down there.

 The problem with this theory: Planes like the Lockheed Electra could float for as long as eight days, especially with the gas tanks empty. Amelia and Fred had inflatable life vests, an inflatable raft, and a pistol that could shoot rockets. Why didn't anybody spot them?

2. THEY LANDED ON ANOTHER ISLAND.

When they couldn't find Howland, they landed on a nearby island in the Pacific. There are a bunch of them: Gardner Island, Baker Island, the Marshall Islands, the Phoenix Islands. Amelia and Fred became castaways there and died of thirst or starvation.

The problem with this theory: If they landed *anywhere*, somebody would have found the plane, or pieces of it, after all these years. And their bodies would be there too. But those islands were searched, and nothing was found.

3. THEY WERE CAPTURED BY THE JAPANESE.

FRECKLE CREAM

Amelia disappeared a few years before World War II began. Japan controlled many islands in the Pacific. So maybe the Japanese thought Amelia was a spy, and captured her.

In 1990, this TV show called *Unsolved Mysteries* interviewed an old woman from the island of Saipan who claimed she saw Amelia and Fred killed by Japanese soldiers.

 Of course, people can say *anything*. There have been rumors that people found bones, rings, bottles, suspicious grave sites, and shoes that were Amelia's size. Somebody found a can of freckle cream on Nikumaroro Island [called

I'm sorry, I've never seen her before.

MISSING

$REWARD$

Gardner Island in Amelia's time] that Amelia supposedly used. People have also claimed Amelia became Tokyo Rose, an English-speaking woman who made propaganda radio broadcasts for Japan during the war.

 The problem with the Japan theory: There's no evidence that it's true or that Amelia was a spy. And the Japanese, who are now our good friends, say it's not true.

 Also, the Japanese would have been *heroes* if they rescued Amelia and Fred. They had little reason to capture them, and no reason to kill them.

 Everybody got excited in 2017 when a History Channel documentary dug up an old photo of a man and woman sitting on a dock in the Marshall Islands. Supposedly, they were Amelia and Fred. But then some blogger found the same photo in a Japanese travel guide that was printed in 1935—two years before Amelia's flight.

 So much for *that* theory.

In a 1995 episode of Star Trek: Voyager, Amelia was abducted by aliens! That was crazy. But I think the craziest theory about Amelia Earhart was that she faked her death. There was a 1970 book, *Amelia Earhart Lives*, that claimed she moved to New Jersey, got married, and changed her name to Irene Bolam.

I've never flown a plane in my life!

 Do you know who *really* hated that theory? Irene Bolam!

Yeah, she sued the publisher, and the book was taken off the market.

There have been submarine expeditions searching for Amelia's plane. Robert Ballard, who found the *Titanic*, started a search in 2019. He found nothing. Every few years, somebody claims they have found a clue that solves the mystery of Amelia Earhart. But none of them have held up.

Most likely, Amelia's plane is sitting at the bottom of the Pacific right now, waiting for somebody to find it.

CHAPTER 12

Getting Even
MORE Famous

Amelia was world-famous in her lifetime. But after she disappeared, she became a *legend*. Since there's no proof that she died, she sort of lives forever.

Hundreds of books and articles have been written about Amelia. She's in the National Aviation Hall of Fame, the National Women's Hall of Fame, the Motorsports Hall of Fame of America, and the California Hall of Fame.

There's a museum at her birthplace in Kansas. One of her planes is on display at the National Air and Space Museum.

 There are statues, scholarships, and awards in her honor. On her birthday in 1963, the U.S. Postal Service issued an eight-cent airmail stamp with her picture on it.

 There are ships, parks, roads, schools, libraries, bridges, and airports named after Amelia. There's a wildlife sanctuary in Ireland. A dorm at Purdue University. A dam in Massachusetts. A hotel in Germany.

A crater on the *moon* was named after Amelia. And in 1987, when astronomer Carolyn S. Shoemaker discovered a new asteroid, she named it 3895 Earhart.

There have been songs . . .

+ "Amelia Earhart's Last Flight," by Yodeling Cowboy Red River Dave McEnery. It was the first song ever performed on TV, at the 1939 World's Fair.

+ "Amelia" was on Joni Mitchell's album *Hejira*.

+ *In Search of Amelia Earhart* was a 1972 tribute album by Plainsong.

There have been movies and TV shows . . .

- *Flight to Freedom* was a 1943 film about a pilot like Amelia who volunteers for a secret government mission. She disappears on purpose to give the Navy a reason to search the islands near Japan.

- *Amelia Earhart: The Final Flight* was a 1994 movie starring Diane Keaton.

- In 2009, Amelia was a character in two movies: *Amelia* with Hilary Swank and *Night at the Museum 2*.

COMING SOON

Amelia

She's even been in video games—*Fortnite Battle Royale* and *The Simpsons: Hit & Run*. In 2018, Amelia got the ultimate honor— Mattel introduced three new Barbie dolls based on inspirational women. One of them was Amelia.

Barbie
Amelia
Earhart

Amelia Earhart

"The stars seemed near enough to touch and never before have I seen so many. I always believed the lure of flying is the lure of beauty, but I was sure of it that night."

CHAPTER 13

Oh Yeah? (Stuff About Earhart That Didn't Fit Anywhere Else)

 When she wasn't flying, Amelia liked to listen to classical music, play piano and banjo, and work in her garden.

 Amelia didn't drink coffee or tea. She liked hot chocolate, buttermilk, and tomato juice. To stay alert during long flights, she kept a bottle of smelling salts.

Amelia was really thrifty. When she stayed in a hotel, she would take all the stationery from the room.

 Amelia was good friends with First Lady Eleanor Roosevelt. When they met in 1932, Eleanor had already flown in an airplane, rode an Olympic bobsled, and learned how to shoot a rifle from the National Guard. Amelia was going to give her flying lessons, and Eleanor even got a student permit. But her husband, President Franklin Roosevelt, talked her out of it.

"The most difficult thing is the decision to ACT."

 After she disappeared, many female pilots honored Amelia by duplicating her last flight. In 2014, a thirty-one-year-old from Denver became the youngest woman to fly around the world in a single-engine plane. Her name—and this is *not* a joke—was Amelia Rose Earhart.

 Amelia had lots of "crack-ups" during her career. On one flight from Cleveland to Detroit, she and a copilot ended up in Lake Erie. They had no radio on the plane, so they floated there for three hours until they were rescued.

In one biography, the author Doris L. Rich wrote that there were "at least half dozen better pilots than Amelia."

Amelia's first car was a 1922 Kissel "Gold Bug" Speedster. It was yellow, and she named it "Yellow Peril."

 In the early days of aviation, flights were bumpy and lots of people got airsick. They used rubber mats on the floors of planes instead of carpet because so many people threw up while flying. Will Rogers said he went through one barf bag for every five hundred miles.

Will Rogers, by the way, died in a 1935 plane crash.

Did you ever hear of an autogiro?

No. What's that?

It was a cross between a plane and a helicopter. They could take off and land without a runway, and they were popular in the 1930s.

Sounds cool.

 Amelia was the first woman to pilot an autogiro, and she set an altitude record, taking one up to 18,415 feet. She wrote an article for *Cosmopolitan* titled "Your Next Garage May House an Autogiro." It predicted that someday families would have landing areas on their front lawn.

 So I'm guessing that never happened.

 No. Autogiros weren't much faster than cars, they were hard to fly, you had to fill the gas tank every two hours, and they weren't safe. Amelia cracked up two of them herself.

Hey, look! I think we finished the book! This is the last page, so it must be done.

Wait. One more thing. Did you know that Bluetooth technology was named after the tenth century Viking King Harald Bluetooth?

What does that have to do with Amelia Earhart?

Nothing. I just thought it was a cool fact.

You're impossible!

TO FIND OUT MORE...

Did we get you interested in the life of Amelia Earhart? Yay! You can watch dozens of videos about her on YouTube and there are lots of other books for kids about her too.

Hey! Wait for me!

ACKNOWLEDGMENTS

Thanks to Simon Boughton, Kristin Allard, Liza Voges, and Nina Wallace. The facts in this book came from many books, videos, websites, and other sources. Especially helpful were *Amelia Earhart: A Biography* by Doris L. Rich, and *East to the Dawn: The Life of Amelia Earhart* by Susan Butler.

ABOUT THE AUTHOR

Dan Gutman has written many books for young readers, such as the My Weird School series, The Genius Files, Flashback Four, *The Kid Who Ran for President*, *The Homework Machine*, *The Million Dollar Shot*, and his baseball card adventure series. Dan and his wife, Nina, live in New York City. You can find out more about Dan and his books by visiting his website (www.dangutman.com) or following him on Facebook, Twitter, or Instagram.

TITLES IN THE

Wait! **WHAT?**

SERIES

Albert Einstein Was a Dope?

Muhammad Ali Was a Chicken?

Amelia Earhart Is on the Moon?

Teddy Roosevelt Was a Moose?